How People Learned to Fly

by Fran Hodgkins •illustrated by True Kelley

Collins

An Imprint of HarperCollinsPublishers

A special thanks to Colonel Neal Barlow,
Professor of Aeronautics at the United States Air Force Academy, for his time and expert review of the book.

The Let's-Read-and-Find-Out Science book series was originated by Dr. Franklyn M. Branley,
Astronomer Emeritus and former Chairman of the American Museum–Hayden Planetarium, and was formerly
co-edited by him and Dr. Roma Gans, Professor Emeritus of Childhood Education, Teachers College, Columbia University.
Text and illustrations for each of the books in the series are checked for accuracy by an expert in the relevant field.
For more information about Let's-Read-and-Find-Out Science books, write to HarperCollins Children's Books,
10 East 53rd Street, New York, NY 10022, or visit our website at www.letsreadandfindout.com.

Library of Congress Cataloging-in-Publication Data

Hodgkins, Fran.
How people learned to fly / by Fran Hodgkins ; illustrated by True Kelley.— 1st ed.
p.   cm.— (Let's-read-and-find-out science book)
ISBN-10: 0-06-029558-9 (trade bdg.) — ISBN-13: 978-0-06-029558-5 (trade bdg.)
ISBN-10: 0-06-445221-2 (pbk.) — ISBN-13: 978-0-06-445221-2 (pbk.)
1. Flight—Juvenile literature. I. Kelley, True. II. Title. III. Series.
TL547.H6165 2007
629.13—dc22

2006000482
CIP
AC

Typography by Rachel L. Schoenberg
11   12   13   SCP   10   9   8   7   6   5   4
❖
First Edition

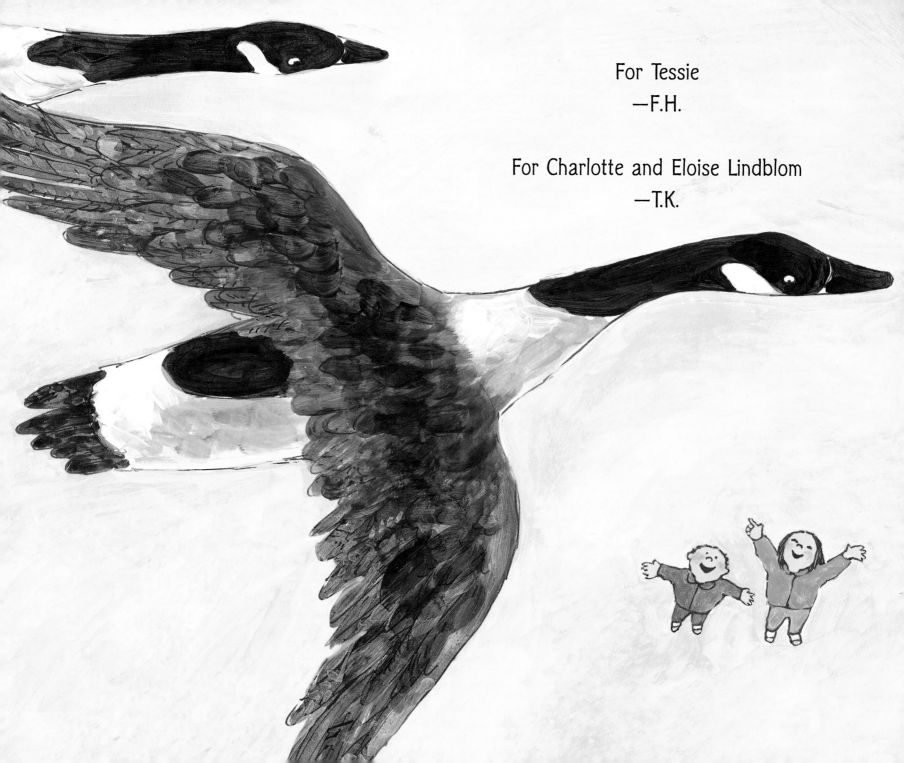

For Tessie
—F.H.

For Charlotte and Eloise Lindblom
—T.K.

When you see a bird flying,
do you dream about flying too?

Do you run with your arms out, imagining that you're soaring among the clouds? Do you make paper airplanes? Do you fly kites?

If you do, you aren't alone. For thousands of years, people have dreamed of being able to fly.

They watched birds and bats soar.

ICARUS

PEGASUS

They imagined people and other animals
that could fly and told stories about them.

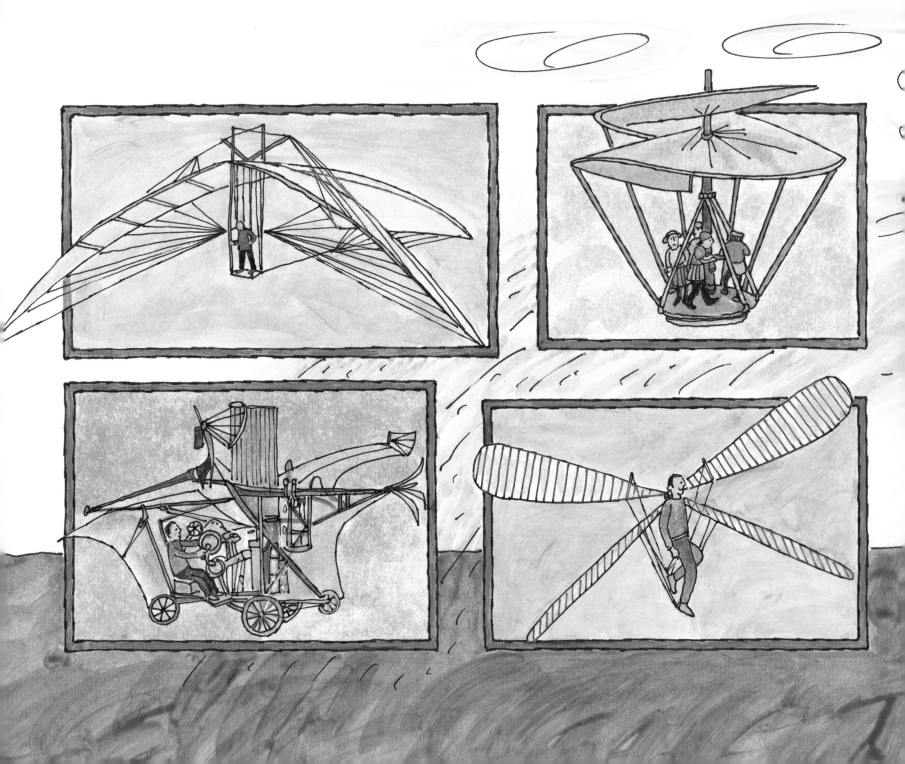

They designed machines that they thought would be able to fly.

They had many ideas. As they tried each new idea, they learned a lot.

They learned about gravity. Gravity is the force that keeps everything on Earth's surface. Because of gravity, things have weight.

If there were no gravity, people, dogs, cats, and everything else would go floating off into space. Gravity keeps us on the ground, even if we would rather be flying.

People also learned about air. Air is made of tiny particles called molecules. When you walk or run, you push through air molecules. They push back on you, too, even though you don't usually feel the push unless the wind blows.

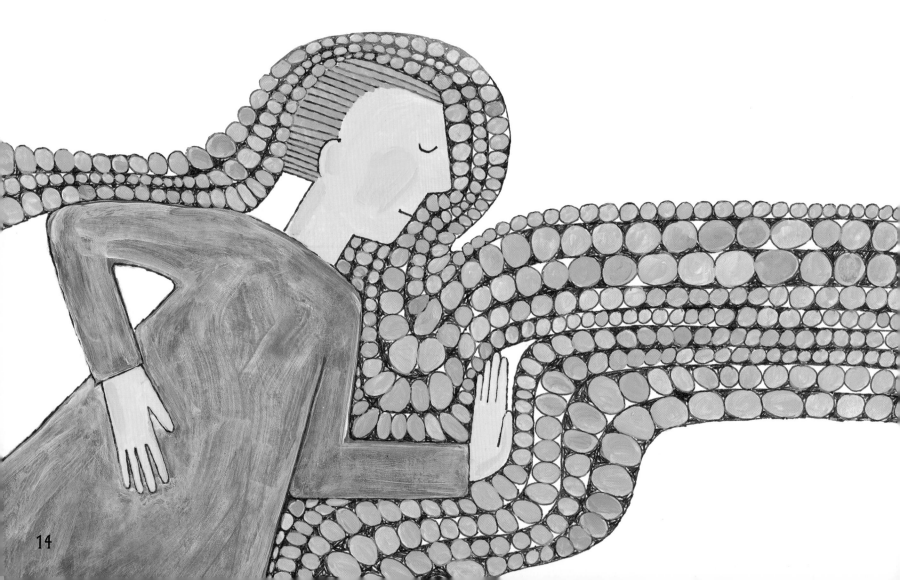

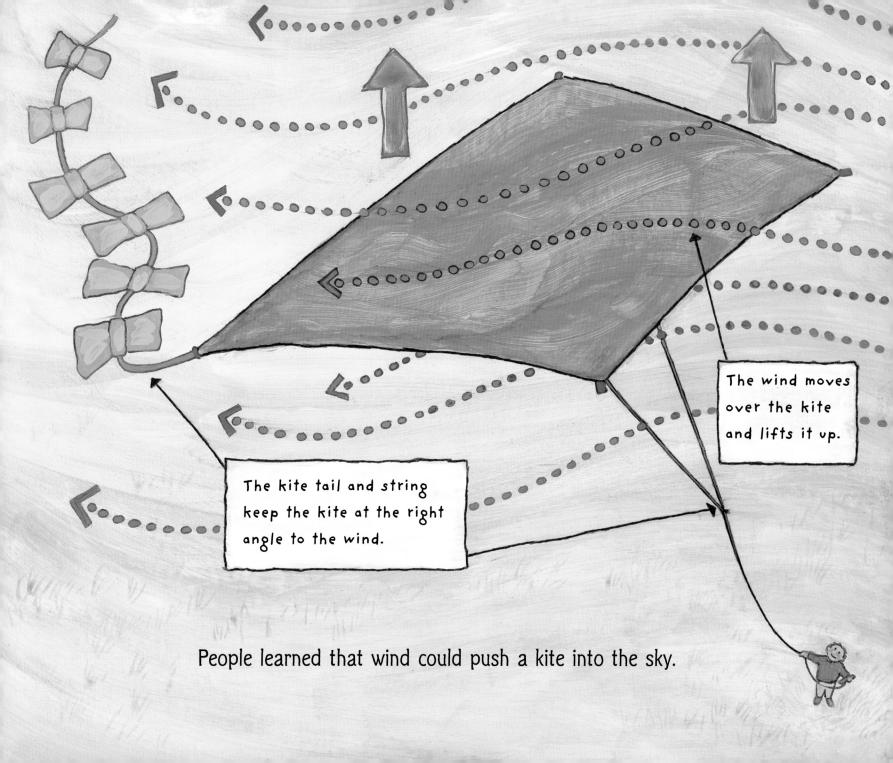

The wind moves over the kite and lifts it up.

The kite tail and string keep the kite at the right angle to the wind.

People learned that wind could push a kite into the sky.

When air molecules push back on a moving object, that is a force called drag. You can feel drag for yourself. Hold out your arms. Now spin around. Feel the push of air on your arms and hands? That's drag. Like gravity, drag works against objects that are trying to fly.

DRAG

Kites were useful and fun, but people wanted more. They wanted to fly like birds.

Birds had something that kites didn't:
Birds had wings.

People made wings and strapped them to their arms. They flapped their arms but couldn't fly.

In England, Monk Elimer broke his legs in A.D. 1010 after a 15-second flight.

They built gliders, light aircraft with wings. Some didn't work, but some did.

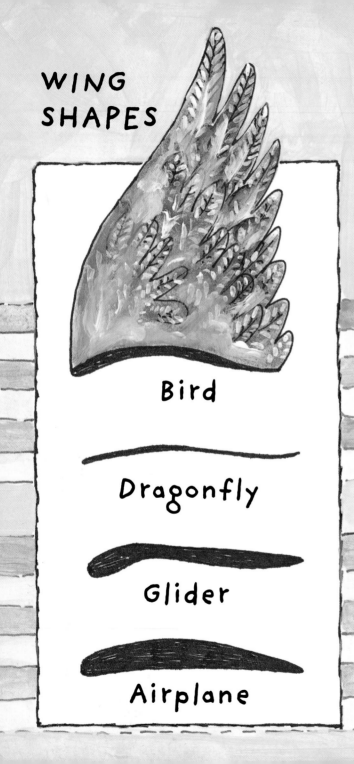

WING SHAPES

Bird

Dragonfly

Glider

Airplane

The gliders that worked best had special wings. These wings were arched on both the top and the bottom. The air pulled the wings from above and pushed the wings from below. When the wings went up, so did the glider! Arched wings help create a force called lift. Lift is the force that keeps birds and gliders in the air.

Most gliders have long, thin wings. The wings create enough lift to carry the aircraft and its passengers. Gliders usually ride currents of air the same way a hawk soars.

Gliders are very light, and long wings and air currents can give them enough lift to fly. But to carry more than just a passenger or two, an aircraft needs a lot more lift. The question is: How do you create more lift?

An engine is the answer!

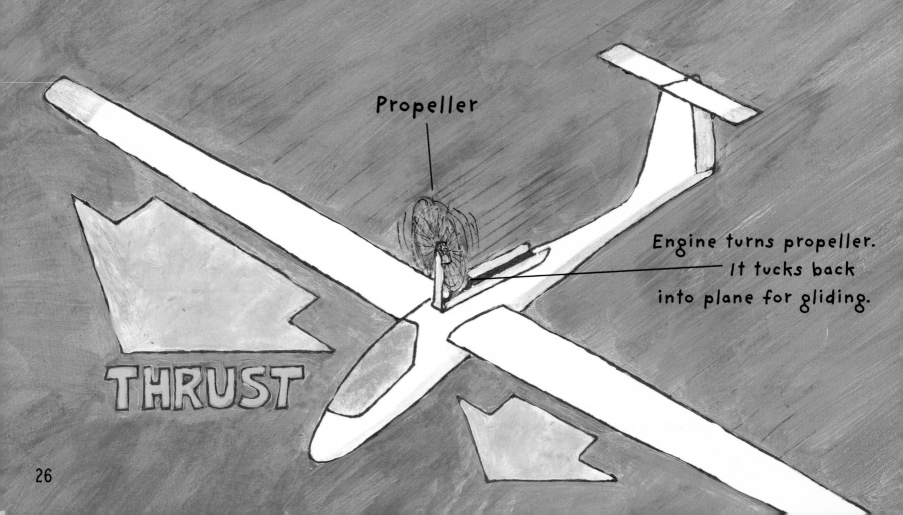

Propeller

Engine turns propeller.
It tucks back
into plane for gliding.

THRUST

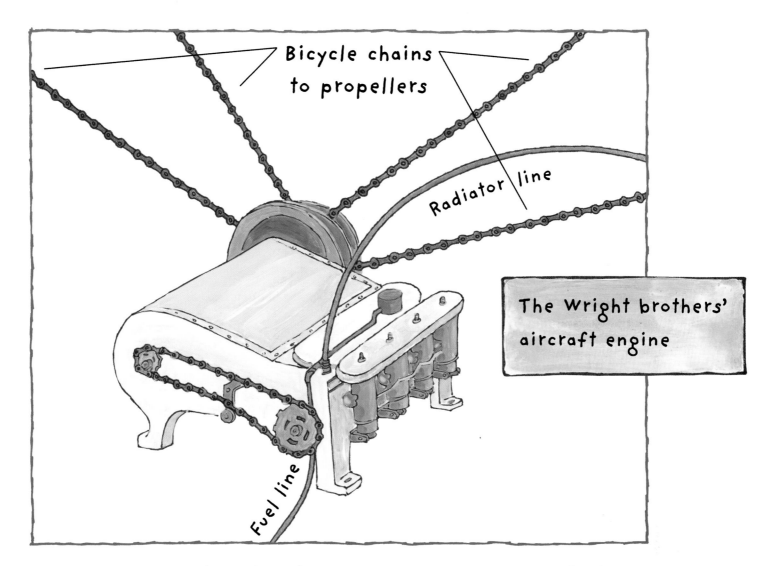

Bicycle chains to propellers

Radiator line

Fuel line

The Wright brothers' aircraft engine

An engine is a machine that changes energy into movement. The forward movement that an airplane needs to fly is called thrust. More thrust makes an airplane move forward faster. Moving faster creates more lift. And with more lift, an airplane can carry more weight. So an aircraft with an engine can carry passengers or cargo.

In 1903 the Wright brothers figured out how to get wings and an engine to work together in order to give an airplane enough thrust to fly. They made the first powered flight at Kitty Hawk, North Carolina.

Supersonic
fighter jet

Since then, people have made airplanes that can fly faster than sound can travel. They have made airplanes that can fly all the way around the world without stopping.

The Voyager

Today, thousands and thousands of people travel in airplanes every day. People really have learned how to fly!

FIND OUT MORE ABOUT FLYING

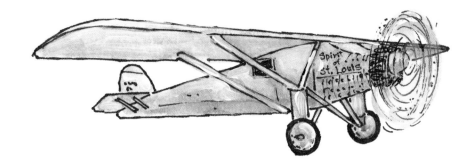

Flying Facts

★ Orville and Wilbur Wright were the first men to build and fly an airplane successfully. In 1903 their Wright Flyer rose into the air at Kitty Hawk, North Carolina.

★ Charles Lindbergh was the first person to fly solo nonstop across the Atlantic Ocean. In 1927 he flew from New York to Paris. His plane was called the *Spirit of St. Louis*.

★ Amelia Earhart was the first woman to fly across the Atlantic Ocean. In 1928 she was one of the three-person crew that made the flight. She became the first woman to fly alone across the Atlantic in 1932.

★ The world record for the longest hand-launched paper-airplane flight is held by Ken Blackburn. In 1998 his paper airplane flew for 27.6 seconds in the Georgia Dome.

Flight School

It's time for you to try your hand at aviation design. By testing a paper airplane inside your house and outside, you can answer questions about flight. You will face the same issues that the Wright brothers faced at Kitty Hawk. Ask one of your friends to help you with this experiment.

Materials needed:

★ Several sheets of 8½-by-11-inch paper ★ Stopwatch ★ Pencil and notebook

Follow the diagram below to build your paper airplane.

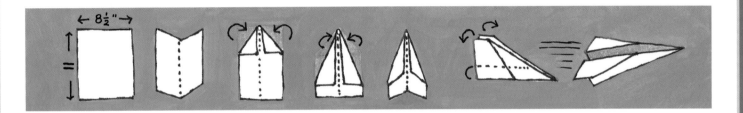

Got your plane made? Good! Then find a long hallway or big open room in your house. Throw the airplane overhand. As soon as it leaves your hand, have your friend start the stopwatch. Stop the timer once the plane falls to the ground. How long does your paper airplane stay in the air? Repeat this experiment several times and write down the times in your notebook. Switch with your friend and let him or her throw the plane while you time its flight. When you switched jobs, were the times different?

Next, try this experiment outside. Is there any wind blowing? Throw the plane into the breeze (when the wind is hitting your face), and then try throwing the plane with the breeze (when the wind is hitting your back). How did the wind affect the plane's flight?

Once you've finished with your indoor and outdoor experiments, think about how these issues are related to flying a real airplane. Did your plane fly better inside or outside? What things would you have to fix about your paper airplane to make it fly better?